Natural Transitioning
An FTM Alternative

Tristan Skye

[*Second Edition*]

Natural Transitioning: an FTM alternative, Second Edition

Cover Design & Interior Design: Tristan Skye

Printed in the United States of America

First Printing: July 2011
Second Printing: August 2015

Printed on Recycled Paper

ISBN 978-1-329-49101-4

For
The transgender men and women whose
journey ended much too soon. To those who
have fought for equal rights. To those brave
enough to accept themselves for who they truly
are and find peace within.

To my parents for your unconditional love.
It is a gift that I treasure. I know my life has
impacted yours in many ways and I thank you
for defending me and losing family and friends
in the process. I love you both so very much.

To Shy and Lloyd for being the loyal and
dedicated leaders of TQ Nation.

To Frank, a man who has become a brother to
me and has shown me what a true friend is.

Lastly, to my sweetheart. Thank you for giving
me a love I didn't know existed, support beyond
any other and advice that leads me to greater
things. You inspire me and I thank God for you
being by my side daily.

CONTENTS

Transsgender. It's not a dirty word. It's not something to be ashamed of or something to hide. You are beautiful. You have a purpose. You have a destiny. You are not a mistake. You are not alone.

OVERVIEW

Natural Transitioning™ (NT) was founded by Tristan Skye in 2008. In short, it is the process of transitioning from female to male (FTM) by raising the testosterone levels your body naturally produces without injecting testosterone. In this book, you will uncover years of dedicated research and my personal experience developing this alternative method of transitioning.

This guide is your road map for success.

There is an actual science of manipulating your body to produce the results you want. All you need is dedication, will-power and knowledge. It's crucial to know your body and what works for you and against you. I researched natural supplements that would help boost levels of testosterone naturally. Over a trial and error process, I formulated a plan that has worked for hundreds of trans men worldwide. As with Hormone Replacement Therapy (HRT), the speed of this process is dependent on the individual's genetics and how low or high their T levels are to begin with. Some may have results faster than others. Also, it's a 3-step process. If you choose only to do 1 or 2 of the 3 steps, your results will most likely be limited and slower.

This is a an alternative option for transmen who:
(1) Are waiting to start HRT
(2) Do not want to take synthetic testosterone or are unable to
(3) Have been on *T and want to try a different option

Important Sidenote:
As with T shots, you need to first make an appointment with your physician and get a physical and blood tests to make sure you are able to Naturally Transition.

*T is a slang way of saying "Testosterone"

NATURAL TRANSITIONING Q&A

Q: *How is it natural? I don't think taking all of those pills is healthy or any different than injecting T.*

A: It is called "natural" because it is a way of increasing your body's natural production of testosterone instead of injecting synthetic testosterone into your body in order to increase T levels. The body naturally produces testosterone in both males and females in the adrenal glands. Cisgender women produce testosterone in their ovaries - a smaller level compared to the testosterone production in cisgender males. Increasing testosterone naturally isn't a new concept. Bodybuilders and athletes have mastered this method over the course of many years with proven results.

Most people who encounter negative side effects over-use supplements and exceed the recommended dosage.

If you experience negative side effects from the regular dosage, then you need to be immediately checked out by your physician. If your body cannot handle the slower, lower levels of T increase with Natural Transitioning, then your body may be unable to handle T injections, gels, creams, pellets or patches.

Natural Transitioning, as in any type of hormone replacement method, is not 100% healthy, yet it is healthier because it is a slower process that leaves the person in more control and able to monitor their changes and transformation. It is not synthetic hormones, but simply an increase in your natural testosterone production.

If you follow the NT guidelines, you will get results. This is only a method to offer an alternative for FTMs. For some, it is the only hope they have to transition.

I believe that there is no "right" way to transition. Each person has to do what is best for them. We have the freedom of choice over our bodies. I'm not against any form or method of transitioning as long as it has been approved first by a medical professional.

Q: *Has this been approved by any physician or medical professional?*

A: Actually, yes. Natural Transitioning was approved for me by a medical professional - the same as one would need a physician's approval prior to taking other forms or methods. Before any type of transition process of HRT, you have to get a physical and blood work to make sure your body is in a healthy enough state and condition to handle the T boosting effects. During your transition, you need to continue to remain under a physician's care and to also monitor your T levels via blood tests.

NT has also been approved by numerous naturopathic doctors (NDs) in both the United States and Canada. These doctors primarily focus on homeopathic remedies that are 100% natural. Many forms of this practice rely on Chinese medicine that has been proven for centuries.

This is also a process of knowing your body and what effects it in different ways. Some things I initially took, I no longer take because I didn't like the effects. I enjoy being able to pick and choose based on how it effects my body and my moods.

How I transition is a choice. Just as you have your choice, I have my choice and everyone else has their choice. There is no need for a debate or trying to prove one method is better than the other. What is best for me may not be best for you. What's best for you may not be best for another trans man.

Q: *I only see positives about NT, I never see the negatives. I just think it's too easy to get DHEA and other stuff and people take it too lightly.*

A: I agree. There wasn't much out there about this back in my first edition of this book. Today, it's not a secret and you can do plenty of research freely on the internet and view different medical publications. I have personally addressed both positives and negatives with my experience and effects. I have also always advised people to be under a physician's care and not to exceed the recommended dosage. It is easy to get because they are natural supplements and many are found online. The source of the supplements is vital. You have to be careful the same as taking anything over the counter. Some guys just don't follow the rules and obviously their health is not important. I have friends who doubled up on their T shots, which is very unhealthy.

We can't monitor anyone but ourselves.

Love yourself more than anything else in the world. Live well. Be well.

ALL ABOUT SUPPLEMENTS

When people think of prescription drugs, most think "artificial." When people think of vitamin supplements, most think "natural."

But both drugs and supplements can be artificial or natural. Many vitamin supplements produced today are artificial. Poison hemlock, hallucinogenic mushrooms, rhubarb leaves and sprouted kidney beans are all natural – and potentially deadly.

There are six categories of nutrients used in the manufacturing of vitamin supplements:

1. NATURAL SOURCE

These include nutrients from vegetable, animal or mineral sources. But before making it into the supplement bottle, they undergo significant processing and refining. Examples include vitamin D from fish liver oils, vitamin E from vegetable oils and natural beta-carotene.

When a vitamin is marked "natural", it only has to include 10% of actual natural plant-derived ingredients. The other 90% could be synthetic.

Consider vitamin E tocopherols, which can be extracted from vegetable oils (often soybean, due to low costs). First, the soybeans are crushed and the protein is removed by precipitation. Second, the resultant oil is distilled off to become bottled vegetable oil. Third, the remaining materials are solubilized to remove any carbohydrates. Fourth, the vitamin E is extracted away from the remaining waxes and lecithin (fatty substance found in animal and plant tissues).

Synthetic alpha-tocopherol is a combination of eight isomers, natural alpha-tocopherol is just one isomer and consuming various isomers can decrease bioavailability. An isomer is a molecule with the same formula as another molecule, but different chemical structure.

2. NATURE-IDENTICAL SYNTHETIC

This includes nutrients completely manufactured in a lab with the molecular structure identical to the same nutrients occurring in nature. Manufacturers often prefer this process because of the cost and scarcity of natural resources. Most standard vitamin supplements on the market today are this type.

An example here would be vitamin C. Most vitamin C currently manufactured is synthetic, coming from China. Vitamin C is a weak acid. Many supplements use salt forms (sodium ascorbate, calcium ascorbate, magnesium ascorbate) to decrease acidity.

The most popular form of synthetic vitamin C is ascorbic acid. Naturally occurring vitamin C is the same molecule as synthetic ascorbic acid. But in food, ascorbic acid is found within the vitamin C complex among other compounds. The ascorbic acid in supplements is often derived from corn starch, corn sugar, or rice starch, and is chemically dependent upon volatile acids.

The method for vitamin C synthesis using two-step fermentation was developed by China in the 1960s.

3. STRICTLY SYNTHETIC

These nutrients are manufactured in a lab and are different than the same nutrients found in nature. Synthetic vitamins can have the same chemical constituents, but still have a different shape (optical activity). This is important because some of the enzymes in the human body only work properly with a vitamin of the correct shape. When we give the body concentrated forms of synthetic nutrients, it doesn't always appear to have an appropriate delivery system.

Starting materials for strictly synthetic supplements can be anything from coal tar to petroleum to acetylene gas. These supplements are made in facilities via chemical manipulations with the goal of duplicating the structure of the isolated vitamin. Specific formulas for the process aren't made available to the public (sorry, I tried).

An example is vitamin B1. Coal tar is a widely used foundational substance for this vitamin — typically a crystalline yellow coal tar (yes, this means it's from coal, a fossil fuel). Hydrochloric acid is often added to allow precipitation. Then fermentation, heating, cooling and other steps are completed until a final synthetic vitamin is created. It's then dried and tested for purity before being shipped to distributors.

Now, to get a natural vitamin B1 supplement the process is quite different.

The food or botanical containing the desired vitamin is harvested and cleaned (let's say wheat germ). It's then placed in a vat to be mixed with water and filtered to create an extract and remove fiber (unlike in whole foods, where you want fiber). The post-filtration extract of the sourced food contains the nutrients found in the original whole food. It's then dried and ready for packaging.

4. FOOD CULTURED

This involves the same process behind cultured foods like yogurt, kefir, miso and sauerkraut. Nutrient supplements are often grown in yeast or algae. Culturing in and of itself creates nutrients and can make them more bioavailable.

Raw materials (minerals and some synthetic nutrients) are added to yeast/algae suspensions where they concentrate within cells. The yeast/algae are then harvested, ruptured and made into a vitamin supplement. The theory here is that yeast/algae contain the nutrients they're fed in a whole food complex.

Sometimes food cultured vitamins are combined with synthetic vitamins to increase potency (i.e. to bump up the milligram/microgram count on the label), since most have a low potency on their own. Remember, counting the milligrams of a synthetic vitamin might not be comparable to what's found in whole foods.

5. FOOD BASED

One kind of food based supplement is made by enzymatically reacting synthetic and natural vitamins with extracts containing vegetable proteins and then making this into a supplement. This is not food cultured, because the nutrients are not grown into a whole food, as in the yeast/algae suspensions.

Manufacturers don't often use concentrates or extracts derived from whole food sources because of low nutrient potency, fluctuating nutrient levels and limited shelf life. Nutrients are easily degraded by heat, pH changes, light and oxygen.

6. BACTERIAL FERMENTATION

This includes nutrients produced by genetically altering bacteria. Genetically altered bacteria can produce nutrient by-products.

Examples include CoQ10, amino acids, ergocalciferol (vitamin D2), menaquinone (vitamin K2), riboflavin (fermentation of ribose), cyancobalamin (vitamin B12; this is exclusively obtained via fermentation processes, as the naturally occurring source of B12 is bacterial metabolic activity - think animal tissues/meat carrying bacteria) and melatonin.

For instance, vitamin D2 is made by artificially irradiating fungus. It's not a naturally occurring form of vitamin D. The starting material is ergosterol, a type of plant sterol derived from fungal cell membranes. Ergosterol is turned into viosterol by ultraviolet light, and then converted into ergocalciferol (vitamin D2).

If you read this entire chapter, you get an A+ and a pat on the back.

ALL ABOUT DHEA

Dehydroepiandrosterone (DHEA) is a natural steroid and precursor hormone produced by the adrenals. You see, testosterone is naturally produced in men and women in the adrenal glands. The adrenal glands are small glands located on top of each kidney. They produce hormones that you can't live without, including sex hormones and cortisol. Cortisol helps you respond to stress and has many other important functions. Our bodies make DHEA naturally - on average around 25mg per day.

For cisgendered men over 30 years of age, they are usually prescribed 50-100mg per day since that is the age DHEA levels begin to decline. For transgender males, 100-150mg daily is recommended to help boost testosterone levels.

Evidence suggests that DHEA may help treat depression, obesity and osteoporosis. However, more research is needed to support its use for hormonal disorders, sexual function and lupus (an autoimmune disorder that affects the skin and organs). DHEA has been studied for the treatment of HIV, schizophrenia and severe injury.

DHEA may cause side effects related to other hormones. Side effects may include symptoms such as oily skin, increased hair growth, a deep voice, irregular periods, smaller breast size and increased genital size. Other side effects that may occur in either sex include acne, sleep problems, headache, nausea, skin itching and mood changes.

Athletes and other people use DHEA to increase muscle mass, strength, and energy. But DHEA use is banned by the National Collegiate Athletic Association (NCAA).

It is not suggested for regular use without a health professional's care.

TESTOSTERONE BOOSTING SUPPLEMENTS

Zinc

Zinc deficiency is extremely widespread throughout the world and even a mild deficiency will quickly lower your serum testosterone levels.

A low zinc diet stops the pituitary gland from being able to release the luteinising and follicle stimulating hormones that stimulate testosterone production.

In one rodent study, a diet that supplied inadequate zinc reduced the number of androgen receptor sites by 40 percent. Estrogen receptor sites increased by 60 percent.

A mild zinc deficiency will reduce the number of androgen binding sites. The unbound testosterone in the blood stream then becomes converted to estrogen in the liver - at the same time the number of estrogen receptors increases. This is extremely bad news.

Zinc fights excess estrogen! This is extremely good news.

Zinc is a powerful aromatase inhibitor that will greatly reduce the conversion of testosterone to estrogen in the body.

When we don't get enough zinc, we begin to experience weakened sex drive, reduced muscle mass, lower energy levels and increased body fat (alongside other problems).

One of the best ways trans men can naturally boost T levels is to make sure they eat a high zinc diet so that estrogen levels in the body are reduced.

D-Aspartic Acid (DAA)

This amino acid plays a critical role in sperm cell and sex hormone production. Research has shown that D-Aspartic acid may enhance luteinizing hormone and testosterone by 46% and 45.5% respectively, in only 13 days. An almost 50% increase in testosterone in less than 2 weeks is very impressive.

Also, animal studies have shown that D-Aspartic acid can boost the levels of Human Growth Hormone (HGH) using the same pathways that HGH is produced in humans.

So as you can see, D-Aspartic Acid can help you to:

+ Boost your testosterone levels safely and naturally
+ Keep your estrogen low
+ Ensure the protein you consume is used to pack on muscle

Vitamin D

Vitamin D is an essential nutrient and we normally produce it from exposure to sunlight. It is made in the skin when 7-dehydrocholesterol reacts with ultraviolet light. However, if you live in the UK or other colder countries, you may be deficient in vitamin D due to minimal exposure to direct sunlight.

A recent study in the *European Journal of Endocrinology* tested vitamin D and hormone levels in 3,051 European men aged 40 to 79. The researchers discovered that men with vitamin D deficiency had significantly lower free testosterone and higher levels of oestradiol and leutenizing hormone, which can indicate hypogonadism and poor reproductive health. Hypogonadism is a condition where the body doesn't produce enough testosterone in cisgender men.

Vitamin D can support hormone production as there are receptors for this vitamin in the hypothalamus and pituitary glands, which produce hormones involved in metabolic and sexual health. Remember that sexual health is directly related to testosterone production.

Oyster Extract

Oysters are very important when it comes to raising testosterone because they are one of the very best sources of zinc, containing 10x the zinc found in beef steak. And if you want healthy testosterone levels, remember that zinc is essential.

Importantly, oyster extract not only contains high levels of zinc, but also all 59 trace elements needed by the body, including vitamins, amino acids, taurine, omega 3 & 6 fish oils, along with zinc's co-factors copper and manganese in a natural, balanced form. These are essential because taking zinc on its own can lead to imbalances in these trace elements.

A lack of zinc can also cause overtraining as your hormones can become unbalanced, causing a lack of muscle and weight gain. Its huge vitamin, mineral and trace element profile will support your body and health in so many ways. In fact, it's a testosterone boosting, multi vitamin/mineral in one supplement.

Ginseng

The herb Ginseng has also been shown to increases the body's production of testosterone when taken regularly. It increases the sex hormones known to stimulate cell growth and boost testosterone levels.

Ginseng also raises the levels of adrenocorticotropic hormone (ACTH) and adrenaline in the body, as low levels of these 2 hormones are believed in turn to cause low testosterone levels.

Fenugreek

Fenugreek is a herb and a spice commonly found as an ingredient in curries. Australian researchers at the University of Queensland working with colleagues at Applied Science and Nutrition (ASN) found in a double-blind, randomized, placebo-controlled study, that daily supplements containing an extract from fenugreek appeared to enhance male libido and normalize testosterone levels. Fenugreek seeds contain bioactive compounds called saponins, including one called diosgenin, which research suggests may be involved in the production of a number of sex hormones.

Magnesium

Another essential nutrient, the mineral magnesium is needed by over 300 different enzymes and is also responsible for a host of processes in the body, including muscle and nerve relaxation, which are very important when you are working out.

Without sufficient magnesium, calcium can overactivate the nerve, sending too many messages to the muscles causing muscle fatigue, tension, soreness, cramps and spasms.

Magnesium deficiency is another widespread problem in our country. While this makes you prone to stress and muscle cramps, it also starves your body's endocrine system of a vital mineral it needs for testosterone production.

Magnesium oxide is the worst and it's very common for magnesium supplements. Don't take any magnesium with an "ide" ending. Magnesium citrate is far better and becoming more common.

Magnesium is needed for the metabolism of proteins, carbohydrates, and fats. Muscle cells can't store certain fuels unless plenty of magnesium is available.

More importantly, according to an article published in the *Journal of Pharmaceutical and Biomedical Analysis*, it's been found that individulas with more magnesium in their blood seem to have higher amounts of free testosterone.

Vitamin B6

Part of the B group of vitamins, Vitamin B6 is essential for many functions in your body, including testosterone production and regulation.

It helps testosterone levels by stimulating androgen (a steroid hormone that acts as a precursor for testosterone) receptors in your body, making your body produce testosterone. It may also suppress the use of natural estrogen, much like oyster extract, thereby amplifying testosterone production in your body.

Garlic

According to the *Journal of Nutrition*, garlic supplementation "alters hormones associated with protein anabolism by increasing testosterone." That's the goal, right? Go eat some garlic. Garlic is one of the best natural ways to raise testosterone levels because it contains a strong compound called allicin that can increase the levels of the testosterone hormone. Allicin breaks down easily, so make sure you eat real garlic. Do not take supplements that have 0% active allicin left.

L-Glutamine

Glutamine has also been taken to enhance brain function as it fuels two of the brain's most important neurotransmitters: glutamic acid and gamma-aminobutyric acid (GABA). It also assists in nitrogen transportation and reduces toxic build up of ammonia in the brain. It has also been used in the treatment of ADD/ADHD, anxiety and depression. It has also been used in recovery programs to break sugar craving cycles in alcoholics and assist diabetics in the management of sugar cravings. It is also used as an anti-inflammatory in the treatment of autoimmune diseases and preserves Glutathione (important for detoxification and immune support) levels in the liver.

Maca

One of my favorite natural testosterone enhancers is maca, an adaptogenic herb that originates in South America which possesses aphrodisiac and hormonal improvement properties. I usually add maca to my shakes and smoothies.

Maca improves thyroid function which improves overall energy levels, enhances detoxification systems, raises levels of the neurotransmitter dopamine and controls levels of the nasty, testosterone lowering hormone prolactin. When dopamine levels are high, the pituitary gland is instructed to raise testosterone levels.

Tongkat Ali

Tongkat ali (Eurycoma longifolia Jack) is an aphrodisiac herb that has been shown in studies to improve sperm quality and sexual performance in male rats; it has also been shown to increase testosterone levels.

Tongkat ali may be capable of lowering estrogen levels by inhibiting the aromatase enzyme while simultaneously raising luteneising hormone (LH) levels and total testosterone concentration – this would make tongkat ali one of the most effective natural testosterone enhancers available.

Tongkat ali extract is both clinicaly proven to increase your testosterone levels through the production of leydig cells and to increase your free testosterone levels by means of lower SHGB levels.

Tribulus Alatus (T-Alatus)

Not to be confused with its relative, Tribulus Terrestris, this special herb was proved in a study to significantly increase the level of free serum testosterone. Tribulus Alatus is also great for muscle-building and strength enhancement. It also boosts your immune support from its high antioxidant qualities. Tribulus Alatus is said to be slightly more effective than Terrestris because it contains 6 unique steroidal saponins. The dosage is in the range of 350mg to 500mg. Also, make sure is it pure Alatus and not a scaled down extract version.

Sidenote: I no longer advise the use of fat burners and/or weight loss supplements. Many contain ingredients that can be harmful. While you may lose weight, the risks associated with these products are simply not worth it. Stick to a lifestyle of a healthy diet and exercise and you will experience a decrease of fat and increase of lean muscle naturally.

HEALTHY LIVER & KIDNEYS

Tumeric

This yellow root—a cousin of ginger—is a powerful liver protector and liver cell regenerator. It not only helps stimulate enzymes responsible for flushing out toxins (including known carcinogens) from the body, but UCLA research found that turmeric is capable of combating the effects of carcinogens.

Milk Thistle

Milk Thistle is an herbal supplement that detoxifies and protects vital liver functions.

Milk thistle has been used for over 2,000 years as a natural treatment for liver disorders. The plant is known in scientific circles as the Silybum marianum (L.) Gaertner (syn. Cardous marianus), but it is more commonly known as "milk thistle," "St. Mary Thistle," "Holy Thistle" and "Lady's Thistle." It is an herbaceous annual or biennial plant belonging to the Asteraceae family that can grow to be ten feet tall with flowers that are red and purple in color.

Milk thistle gets its name from the milky white fluid that comes from the plant's leaves when they are crushed. It is native to southern Europe, southern Russia, Asia Minor and North Africa, and has also been naturalized to North and South America.

Europeans were among the first to use milk thistle seeds as an herbal treatment for liver disorders. However, the plant's remedial capabilities have been known since ancient times. Milk Thistle was mentioned by Theophrastus in the 4th century B.C. by the name of "Pternix" and it was also referred to by Pliny the Elder in the 1st century A.D. by the name of "Sillybum." Additionally, in 1744, Von Haller documented the specific use of the plant for liver disorders in its "Medizinischen

Lexicon." In more recent years, many authors such as Johann Gottfried Rademacher, Volker Schulz and Henry Leclerc mention the benefits of Silybum Marianum (milk thistle) when used as a treatment of liver diseases as well as in the treatment of disorders of the bile duct and spleen.

Over the past forty years, intensive chemical, pharmacological and clinical research has confirmed the mechanisms of action and therapeutic value of milk thistle in a wide range of human liver-related and non-liver-related conditions. Literally hundreds of modern research studies have confirmed the remarkable ability of milk thistle to protect the liver and the body against virtually all types of damage.

Additionally, the United States National Library of Medicine and the National Institutes of Health (NIH) have cataloged more than 400 scientific studies of milk thistle and its active compounds in their medicine database. These studies reflect what generations past knew and depended on – that milk thistle is one of the most valuable and beneficial herbal remedies and treatments available anywhere in the world.

Today, milk thistle is still one of the most commonly used medicinal plants in the world and is also the number one recommended natural herb for liver health. In fact, in Europe, milk thistle is a prescribed medication. The milk thistle extract is prescribed to treat mushroom poisoning, alcoholic cirrhosis, chronic hepatitis, drug and alcohol-induced liver damage and acute viral hepatitis, just to name a few.

Milk thistle extract is used to maintain liver health and to protect the liver from the effects of toxins such as alcohol, a polluted environment or workplace, and a host of liver related diseases.

Dandelion

Herbalists use dandelion root to detoxify the liver and gallbladder, and dandelion leaves to support kidney function. Dandelion leaves act as a diuretic and increase the amount of urine produced by the body, supporting kidney function. Dandelion leaves are also used to stimulate the appetite and aid digestion.

Having proper kidney function is essential for healthy living. The sesquiterpene lactones (bitter) compounds found in both dandelion leaf and dandelion roots have diuretic effects. This diuretic effect of dandelion leaf is important in cleansing the kidney because it helps to remove toxins from the kidney.

Since dandelion root and dandelion leaf are diuretics and increase the excretion of water from the body, it is important to drink adequate amounts of water to compensate for the water loss. Diuretics cause the body to remove excess sodium and chloride from the body, which are also eliminated from the body through the urine.

The high amount of vitamins, calcium, potassium and other trace minerals in dandelion root and dandelion leaf balances the nutrients removed from the body as a result of dandelion root and leaf's diuretic effects. My personal goal is to drink a gallon of water a day to fight dehydration which can occur because of the water loss caused by this natural diuretic.

Herbalists use dandelion root to increase bile production to break down fats and remove cholesterol from the body. Studies support that dandelion root extract fights liver fibrosis by inactivating hepatic stellate cells, the major cell type involved in liver fibrosis, and by supporting liver health by enhancing hepatic (liver) regenerative capabilities.

The bitter compound taraxacin of dandelion root possesses cholagogue properties which cause the gallbladder to contract to increase bile flow. Bile is fluid that is made and released in the liver and stored in the gallbladder, also aiding with digestion. The buildup of harmful material in the gallbladder can reduce gallbladder contraction which results in less bile being released to break down fats and to remove cholesterol from the body.

NEGATIVE SIDE EFFECTS

When hormones are altered, side effects happen. This occurs whether you are going the natural route or synthetic.

+ WEIGHT GAIN - Increasing testosterone levels doesn't always help you lean down. Sometimes, you get lean and trim at first, but then your body adjusts and you can start gaining weight.

+ MOOD SWINGS - This occurs most frequently using testosterone injections and gels.

+ ACNE - You are basically going through puberty and as a result, your skin produces more oil. Where there is more oil, there is a potential for acne.

+ SWELLING - This usually occurs in the arms and/or legs.

+ HAIR LOSS - This is definitely one that can be devastating to self esteem in some trans men. If you have a family history of androgenic alopecia (male pattern baldness), I recommend that you immediately start using all-natural products to help aid in slowing hair loss and keep your hair follicles stimulated with proper blood circulation. Dihydrotestosterone (DHT) is the main culprit in hair loss. Minoxidil is FDA-approved to help reverse the effects of hair loss. It is not natural, but I do approve of its use. It has magnified results when combined with Emu oil. Stay away from prescription hair loss drugs, such as finasteride.

TESTOSTERONE BOOSTING FOODS

The general rule to keep in mind is that you want to focus on foods that contain more protein and less carbs (think breads, not veggies) and sugar.

Despite what common wisdom claims, eating healthy fats doesn't make you fat, as long as they are natural fats, and not trans-fats. In fact, natural fats can actually help keep you lean. Our bodies were evolved to metabolize natural fats readily. Healthy fats include avocados and nuts. Individuals who choose low-fat diets typically have decreased testosterone levels. Healthy fats are the way to go!

Protein will be your biggest key to gaining muscle and to help your body manufacture more testosterone. Stay away from fried foods, wheat, sugar and salt (substitute with coconut sugar and sea salt). You want a soda? Drink water or tea. Stay away from diet soda. Stay away from diet anything, actually - including low fat and fat free. Instead of using butter in your frying pan, try coconut oil as a healthier alternative. A paleo diet is actually the best diet to help boost testosterone. I also recommend to limit dairy. Try to substitute cow milk for cashew, almond, coconut or hemp milk. This may sound like a food tsunami devasting you right now, but your taste buds will adjust and soon you will enjoy a healthier way to eat. How you look and how you feel will be worth it all.

+ **Beef** - Enjoy that juicy steak. Still go for a leaner cut, but steak is high in protein. Try Bison for a leaner alternative. Make sure to buy grass fed if possible; otherwise, the beef itself may contain hormones that can counteract what you're trying to accomplish.

+ **Chicken and Eggs** - Both are great sources of protein. The white breast meat of chicken is the best. Again, use free range, hormone-free chicken. It may be more expensive, but your health is priceless. Egg yolks are loaded with important vitamins like B1 and B2 and nutrients like lutein which maintain healthy eyes. But, they are also a good source for cholesterol, which, believe it or not, testosterone is produced from. I buy organic eggs and/or cage free.

+ **Seafood** - High in protein, contains basically no carbs, and oysters, in particular, are loaded with the mineral zinc. Zinc has many functions in the body, such as aiding in muscle manufacturing and increasing testosterone levels. If you eat fish, make sure you buy saltwater fish since those are the T boosting "mighty" fish. Lastly, be cautious of mercury levels and only buy wild caught! Never eat farm raised fish and try not to eat fish out of a can.

Believe it or not, there are also non-meat sources that should top your list of the foods that boost testosterone.

Just a couple of these are broccoli, cauliflower, brussel sprouts and cabbage. They contain something called Indole-3-carbinol. Indole-3-carbinol, in simple terms, helps to reduce estrogen.

Garlic is a wonderful herb that contains a potent active ingredient called allicin that helps to increase testosterone. Plus, it keeps away vampires.

Avocados, pumpkin seeds (unsalted, sprouted), sweet potatoes, almonds, green leafy veggies (collards, turnip greens and kale), bok choy (chinese cabbage), basically all forms of cabbage is REALLY good! Olive Oil and mushrooms also boost T levels in the body.

The *Journal of Endocrinology* has determined that soy (which contains phytoestrogens) will decrease testosterone levels. A study performed by the Gifu University School of Medicine located in Japan revealed that testosterone concentrations were inversely related with the intake of soy products; hence, the fear of consuming soy products. Soy products are tricky. Although beneficial generally speaking, the only soy product that helps stimulate testosterone production is soybeans.

This may break your heart, but the hops in beer are so estrogenic, they are currently being studied as a treatment for hot flashes in menopausal women. If you want to optimize your testosterone levels, it's best to completely avoid alcohol. Research has shown that even two drinks per day can lower your T levels. If you really want an alcoholic beverage, try a low-sugar cider or stick with clear liquors such as vodka.

Changing your diet is one of the biggest challenges once you make the decision to improve your health. The majority of people are accustomed to eating highly processed foods on a regular basis and ending this negative cycle can be difficult. The good news is that it isn't impossible and once you make it a habit to eat healthy, it becomes a part of your life and you feel better and live longer.

In a nutshell, eating healthy means staying away from the junk that typically makes up the Standard American Diet (SAD). These types of food include man-made sugar, bad fats (hydrogenated, trans-fat), preservatives, white bread and any other ingredients that are unnecessary. I also avoid gluten even though I am not gluten-intolerant. I am dairy-intolerant and avoid that 90% of the time. An easy way to remember if a food is healthy is: "if man made it, don't eat it."

You need to stay away from all foods that contain GMOs and especially high frutose corn syrup. The only alternative sugar I personally use is Stevia. I stopped using Splenda years ago.

I have to say this one more time: The antibiotics and stress levels in animals not raised in a humane manner can actually cause hormone shifts in your own body. You owe it to yourself, your health and your testosterone to buy grass-fed beef, organic eggs and bacon that is nitrate-free. Chicken needs to be free-range and fish needs to be wild caught, not farm raised. It may be a bit more expensive, but the alternative isn't worth it. Personally, I do not eat pork and I say "NO" to GMO.

Another thing I suggest is to do a 3-day or 10-day juice clease. I did a 10-day juice cleanse and the first 3 days I felt exhausted. Starting on day 4, I felt revitalized and by day 10, I had lost 12 pounds. Your body doesn't want all of the toxins and is happy to get rid of it, but it's up to you to do so. Another tip is to drink a lot of water. I'm sure you're tired of hearing that, but it's true. Water flushes out toxins. I also enjoy herbal teas, especially morrocan mint, green tea and roobias chai.

Memorize the "Dirty Dozen" - (produce that has the most pesticides)

12 Most Contaminated

1. Peaches
2. Apples
3. Sweet Bell Peppers
4. Celery
5. Nectarines
6. Strawberries
7. Cherries
8. Pears
9. Grapes (Imported)
10. Spinach
11. Lettuce
12. Potatoes

12 Least Contaminated

1. Onions
2. Avocado
3. Sweet Corn (Frozen)
4. Pineapples
5. Mango
6. Sweet Peas (Frozen)
7. Kiwi
8. Bananas
9. Cabbage
10. Broccoli
11. Papaya
12. Asparagus

Eating healthy can be a major transition for a majority of people due to addictions to sugar, bread, processed foods and fast food. It takes discipline in order to make eating healthy a habit, but it is possible and has many long-term health benefits.

I cannot emphasize enough the importance of increasing muscle mass and decreasing body fat when it comes to testosterone levels. Adipose tissue (fat tissue) contains an enzyme called aromatase that converts testosterone into estrogen. *The more body fat = more estrogen = less testosterone.* You've heard this before and you may hear it again by the time you finish reading this book.

In my first edition of this book, I was not in tune with a truly healthy eating lifestyle. Over the years, I have read countless books, watched plenty of documentaries and have had discussions with numerous naturopathic doctors. With this new-found knowledge, I cannot stress the importance of making positive food choices. The more alkaline your body becomes, the less likely you are to face diseases in the future, including cancer. It may cost a little bit more, but you can usually find farmer's markets or lower-cost natural grocery stores. I try to buy local as often as possible and if you can grow your own food, definitely do it.

FUN FACT: Always use BPA-free bottles since it may be the biggest culprit to declining levels of testosterone. BPA is Bisphenol-A, a synthetic chemical often found in various plastic containers that leach out once heated. When workers were exposed to BPA, it resulted in lower T levels and androstendione, a precursor to both testosterone and estrogen. Use glass or stainless steel whenever possible.

ALL ABOUT ESTROGEN

In the Natural Transitioning™ Series, I mostly cover everything to help BOOST your natural testosterone levels.

Now, I'd like to address things that will increase estrogen levels. Things you should stay away from. In turn, this will help naturally increase your T levels even more. Pretty logical, wouldn't you say?

Low estrogen levels can lead to the following conditions:

+ Bone loss and osteoporosis
+ Increased LDL ("bad" cholesterol)
+ Decreased HDL ("good" cholesterol)
+ Low blood pressure
+ Hair loss
+ Weight gain
+ Sore joints and muscles
+ Fatigue
+ Gastrointestinal disturbances (including indigestion, gas and bloating)
+ Increase in allergies
+ Depression
+ Anxiety
+ Irritability
+ Insomnia
+ Memory loss
+ Difficulty concentrating

ESTROGEN-RICH FOODS

There are a number of foods that contain natural estrogens including those listed below:

Beans/legumes: black-eyed peas, chickpeas, lentils, lima beans, navy beans, red beans, soybeans and soybean sprouts and split peas.

Fruits: apples, cherries, grapefruit, dates, papaya, plums and pomegranates.

Grains: barley, hops, oats, brown rice and wheat.

Herbs and spices: clover, licorice, parsley and sage.

Seeds: alfalfa, anise, fennel, flax, pumpkin, sesame and sunflower.

Vegetables: beets, carrots, celery, cucumbers, eggplant, peppers, potatoes, rhubarb, tomatoes and yams.

As you will soon find out, some of these are also known T boosters. Confusing? Yes! The ones that elevate both are safe for you to still eat - they basically cancel themselves out.

You can increase your energy, lean muscle mass, sexual energy and reduce your body fat by using combinations of exercise, healthy food and very specific natural herbs. The ultimate key to maintaining a lean physique, without observable body fat on your waistline, is not just about your blood level of testosterone, but it's about estrogen, too. But what they have not all realized is that they do not need synthetic drugs to do it!

Many people have imbalances of estrogen and testosterone and of specific estrogens in both blood and fatty tissues. Too much of specific estrogens in your blood and tissue cause fat gains, slow loss of muscle and the reduction of both sexual performance and drive.

Some trans men may have too much of the wrong kind of estrogen because of artificial synthetic hormone replacement and after being on a high fat, low protein diet. Individuals of all ages under great physical and emotional/mental stress, and specifically if they are older, suffer from decreasing testosterone and high relative estrogen. High estrogen can actually decrease the benefits of testosterone.

Alcohol always makes matters worse by inhibiting your ability to clear estrogen from the blood stream by acting as a central system depressant and also by decreasing zinc. And food? Well, even grapefruit can inhibit your liver's ability to breakdown estrogen. Broccoli and cauliflower may mitigate some effects of some estrogens. Soy products may help your liver metabolize/excrete excess estrogen.

Isoflavones found in soy (like genistein and diadzein) block some receptor sites where estrogen binds to cells. The effect is to prevent estrogen from accumulating in your body. Red grape skin extract (resveratrol) improves the liver P450 system and effectively removes excess estrogen. Vegetables rich in vitamin C like bell peppers and fruit reduce aromatase reductase, the major enzyme responsible for converting androstenedione and testosterone into estrogen.

Di-Indolin is a substance believed to be an active cruciferous substance (broccoli, cauliflower, kale) for promoting beneficial estrogen metabolism. Di-Indolin helps increase, by 75%, the "good" 2 hydroxy estrogens, which have an affinity to bind blood proteins (SHBG). The effect of this is to leave greater levels of free testosterone.

Diindolylmethane also dramatically decreases the "bad" estrogen 16-hydroxyestrone by 50%. This product is for athletes, bodybuilders and individuals taking testosterone who are interested in the best possible control of estrogen to obtain a lean and strong body.

There are indications that chrysin, also called Flavone X, a supplement from the herb passion flower (passiflora coerulea L) derived from vegetables rich in biological flavonoids and quercetin (a very strong anti-oxidant), helps absorb enzymes that catalyze increased estrogen production. Of all the tested theoretical flavone anti-estrogens, chrysin measures as the most favorable.

The mineral zinc inhibits the aromatase enzyme that converts testosterone into excess estrogen. Some trans men, who are not meat eaters and have reduced sexual drive, may increase levels of testosterone with zinc gluconate.

Each mineral has a specific effect and works in balance. Manganese gluconate should be taken with zinc (tropical fruits like mangos and pineapples). Zinc is a bit of a wild card. Zinc has been shown to mitigate the development of colds if taken at first onset. On the other hand, too much zinc can lower your HDL levels of cholesterol. That is not desirable. This is why blood, urine and/or saliva testing should always be recommended by your attending physician.

Fat cells are loaded with aromatase, storing large quantities of estrogen. **The higher your percentage of body fat, the more estrogen you will produce** unless you control your diet and combine supplements and exercise to lower estrogen production. As you reduce stored body fat, your estrogen conversion will be reduced and testosterone levels will naturally increase.

It will actually become easier for you to lose weight with proper hormone balance, correct eating, supplementation and exercise. Fish is high in L-Dopa and helps release dopamine and enhance testosterone levels. And certain forms of fatty fish are high in the favorable omega fish for good heart health. You should eat only small amounts of fatty fish though, as even fish can have undesirable effects on your cholesterol and coronary circulation. Watch your mercury levels when eating fish and always eat wild caught, not farm raised. Fish in a can is not desirable.

Some studies have suggested that the pro-hormone, androstenedione, can boost transient levels of testosterone. Such increased levels might lead to slight increases in strength, muscular size and endurance over time (assuming one lifts weights while experiencing the elevated T levels). However, while a few studies have shown that an oral ingestion of 300 mg of androstenedione can raise testosterone levels, much more than DHEA, other studies strongly suggest that androstenedione conversion can catalyze reversibly and increase estrogen compounds instead.

If you use androstenedione, it should only be taken 30 minutes before training or sex and not more than 2-3 times a week. Likewise, if you are someone of such variability who develops high testosterone production from andro excess, this might also lead to estrogen rebound and the formation of fatty tissue in the male breast. This is, of course, a major problem with users of more potent anabolic steroids as well.

I also believe that androstenediol is the more potent form of prohormone as compared to androstenedione. When combined they can be effective if used two or three times a week. Androstenedione has been banned in some countries and I personally do not use it.

Testosterone, estrogen, progesterone and melatonin are cyclic, going up and down throughout the day, night and month. Saliva tests for free testosterone can be performed with three samples, one in the morning, afternoon and late night. An individual's testosterone level is usually highest in the morning. The levels change every 3 minutes - crazy, but true!

DHEA sulfate is very stable with very little change in levels from day to day. A single saliva test for DHEA can tell you if your levels are below ideal. The addition of DHEA can convert into the necessary testosterone for trans men, as the body needs, but cisgendered men generally do not get much conversion of DHEA to testosterone. In fact, cisgender men tend to get more estrogen conversion from DHEA if they use too much (over 50 mg of DHEA per day). Herbs like Avena Sativa, Maca and Horny Goat Weed may completely restore the free and total testosterone to normal levels in many cases, or help raise levels in our case. I personally use Creatine Monohydrate as part of my weight training routine.

During menopause, women have typically been given small amounts of estrogen and progesterone if needed. Now, they are also starting to give a small amount of testosterone as this replenishes energy, libido, bone and immune strength the same as it does in cisgender males.

As you lose weight and reduce fat in your diet, your levels of bad estrogen will decline. Your body will have less fat to make more of the bad type of estrogen. It's best to take supplements of natural steroid hormones in the morning if you choose to incorporate that in your NT plan. All hormones peak at 4-5 hours after ingestion, then within 24 hours, the levels come back down.

GH - Thyroid - Melatonin

Peptide hormones such as melatonin and growth hormone are usually the opposite of testosterone in that they are highest at night and lowest in the day. It's best to take peptide hormones such as melatonin at night. You need to mimic what the body does, which is to spike or release growth hormone in early morning, afternoon and late at night. Your thyroid also naturally spikes at night in a young, healthy individual. If you take thyroid glandular or a natural prescription (Armour) at night, you might contribute to insomnia.

Take melatonin only at night. Melatonin should drop in the morning and increase at night. If melatonin is too high during the day it can cause you to be lethargic. Daylight will help lower melatonin. If melatonin is too high, you need a sun lamp or outdoor light. Vitamin D3 is a great natural substitute.

Exercise lowers melatonin and this may be another reason to exercise in the morning to enhance energy and alertness. If you exercise at night, it may be necessary to take a supplement of melatonin. One milligram is what the body would naturally produce each night if you were in optimum health.

I usually do my exercise (high intensity, short workouts) in the morning; yet, on the times I exercise at night, I take some melatonin just before bed and it seems to work quite well for me to get deep, rejuvenating sleep. Certain foods that contain melatonin such as rice, ginger, tomatoes and corn also may help you sleep better.

MOVE YOUR BODY

Exercise boosts testosterone in two important ways. First, specific types of exercise actually cause our body to produce more testosterone. Second, exercise helps to increase muscle mass and decrease body fat. As we've discussed previously, adipose tissue converts testosterone into estrogen. The less fat we have, the more T we have.

Lift Weights

If you want to increase testosterone, you've got to start lifting – and lifting heavy. Doing a short circuit with the weight machines won't cut it.

Here's what research says on how to craft your weightlifting routine to maximize testosterone production:

+ Use compound lifts. Squats, bench press, deadlift and shoulder press should be your main lifts. Exercises that work large muscle groups are associated with higher increases in testosterone.

+ Go for high volume. Workout volume is determined by the following formula: Sets x Reps x Weight. Studies suggest that higher volume workouts result in higher T production.

+ Don't take each set to failure. It's okay to push yourself to failure on the very last set, just don't do it for all of your sets.

+ Rest for more than a minute and less than two minutes between each set.

HIIT Training

In addition to weightlifting, studies have shown that HIIT workouts can also help boost testosterone levels. For those of you who don't know, HIIT stands for high-intensity interval training. It calls for short, intense bursts of exercise, followed by a less-intense recovery period. You repeat with the intense/less-intense cycle several times throughout the workout. In addition to increasing T, HIIT has been shown to improve athletic conditioning and fat metabolism, as well as increase muscle strength.

Don't overtrain!

It seems like today it's a badge of honor to train every day until exhaustion. The ethos is to push yourself harder and harder every day. If that's your philosophy towards exercise, you might be sabotaging your testosterone levels. Studies have shown that overtraining can reduce testosterone levels significantly. Yes, it's important to exercise hard, but it's even more important to give your body rest so it can recuperate from the damage you inflicted upon it.

Give yourself at least two days during the week when you don't do any intense exercise at all. Depending on your workouts, more days off might be in order. I typically take the weekends off from intense exercise and go on a light walk or hike instead.

Just move more. I try to be more active throughout the work day. I take breaks every 30 minutes or so to stretch or take a walk.

YES TO SLEEP, NO TO STRESS

Most Americans today are sleep deprived, which may be a contributing factor if you notice declining testosterone levels. Our body makes the most testosterone for the day while we're sleeping. Once your T levels increase, you will most likely experience an increased sexual desire in the morning when you wake up.

But, if you're not getting enough quality sleep, your body can't produce testosterone as efficiently or effectively. In one study, researchers at the University of Chicago found that young men who slept less than five hours a night for one week had lower testosterone levels than when they were fully rested. The drop was typically 10-15%.

Not only does sleep boost T, but it also helps manage cortisol, a stress hormone that has been shown to wreak havoc on testosterone levels when present in high amounts.

Getting only 4 to 5 hours of sleep per night is a total testosterone killer! You need to try to get 8 to 9 hours of sleep at night as consistently as possible. Stop mindlessly surfing the net and close those sleepy eyes.

It's also important to improve the quality of sleep you get. For example, reduce exposure to blue light in the evening. I have a phone app that adjusts the blue light on my phone. You also need to reduce your consumption of caffeine in the evenings. Another tip is to take warm showers before bed. Personally, if I start to read a book (a real book, not an online book), I will quickly drift to sleep. Sometimes I also listen to meditation music which does the trick.

When we face stress, our adrenal glands secrete cortisol to prepare our bodies and minds to handle the stressful situation — the primal fight-or-flight response. In small dosages, cortisol is fine and even useful, but elevated cortisol levels for prolonged periods can do some serious damage to our bodies and minds. One area that seems to take a hit when cortisol is high is our testosterone levels. Several studies have shown a link between cortisol and testosterone. When cortisol levels are high, testosterone levels are low; and when testosterone levels are high, cortisol levels are low.

Going to a really good counselor I think is important for everyone. I advise going to a therapist who specializes with transgender therapy and gender identity. Certainly not to change you, but to help guide you through the process. We all need a safe person that we can rip open our heart and minds open to that will listen and respond with wisdom and love.

Anger, anxiety, stress, depression, self-hatred, guilt, resentment...the list goes on and on. We have all gone through many stages of emotional ups and downs and transitioning is one of the most challenging things you will ever do in your life. You need to express your fears, your hopes and pain. Once you free your inner self and invite peace within, stress will not be able to consume you any longer. Don't attempt to take this journy alone. This is one to find helpful hands to hold by your side. It doesn't make you weak. It actually makes your stronger.

CHEMICAL KILLERS

Avoid Xenoestrogens and other T-Lowering chemicals.

Many endocrinologists are sounding the alarm about the damaging effects that come with exposure to common household chemicals.

Called "endocrine disruptors," these chemicals interfere with our body's hormone system and cause problems like weight gain and learning disabilities. One type of endocrine disruptor is particularly bad news for our testosterone levels.

Xenoestrogen is a chemical that imitates estrogen in the human body. When men are exposed to too much of this estrogen-imitating chemical, T levels drop significantly. The problem is xenoestrogen is virtually everywhere — plastics, shampoos, gasoline, cows, toothpaste - you name it and chances are there are xenoestrogen in it. The ubiquitous nature of this chemical in our modern world is one reason some endocrinologists believe that testosterone levels are lower in men today than in decades past. It's also a reason doctors say the number of boys born with hypospadias — a birth defect in which the opening of the urethra is on the underside of the penis and not at the tip — has doubled. Note to expecting parents: make sure mom stays away from xenoestrogens during the pregnancy.

This is how I personally avoid products that contain xenoestrogens:

+ Stored food in glassware and never, ever, ever heated food in plastic containers. Most modern plastics contain phthalates. Phthalates are what give plastic their flexibility, durability and longevity. But, they also screw with hormones by imitating estrogen. Because I do not want any of those T-draining molecules in my food, I keep all my food in glassware. I also made sure to never heat food in plastic containers, as heat increases the transfer of phthalates into food.

+ Avoid exposure to pesticides and gasoline. Sure the smell of gas is manly, but it contains xenoestrogen. Same goes for pesticides. Limit your exposure to these products. If you do come in contact with them, make sure to wash your hands thoroughly. If you have to use pesticides, wear a mask that covers your nose and mouth. When you pump gasoline, walk away from it while your tank is being filled.

+ Eat organic when possible. Pesticides and hormones that are used in our food can imitate estrogens in our body. If budget doesn't allow, at least make sure to wash your fruits and veggies before eating. You can buy a special spray for fruits and veggies that will specifically remove harmful residues. Buy local, if possible, and find meat and milk that comes from cows that haven't been treated with hormones or antiboitics.

+ Use natural grooming products. Most grooming products these days contain parabens, another type of xenoestrogen. And by most, I mean more than 75% of all products. To reduce my exposure as much as possible, I became a hippy during my experiment and started using all natural, paraben-free grooming products. You can find most of these items at most health food stores.

DEEPEN YOUR VOICE

Once your voice stretches, lengthens and deepens, it cannot be reversed. This is great news for trans men. When it comes to deep voice training, you have to be very persistent. By training your voice, you can make it sound richer and deeper. Sidenote: many trans men who are singers are thrilled when they speak deeper, but vocally, it takes adjustment.

I'm going to share three voice training tips that over time, will help deepen the sound of your voice and improve resonance.

Remember, the key to a successful deep voice training program is to perform these exercises consistently!

Neck muscle exercises

This may sound silly, but stronger neck muscles can actually help. They don't directly effect the sound of your voice, but they will relieve vocal cord tension, lower voice pitch and improve resonance.

Posture Exercises

Posture plays a large role when it comes to the sound of your voice. If your chin is down and you are constantly in a slouched position your voice will suffer. Simply by sticking your chest out and lifting your chin, you will immediately notice an improvement in voice depth.

Daily Voice Exercises

Humming while slowly raising and lowering your chin helps loosen tense vocal cords and lowers voice pitch over time. To find the "sweet spot", start by humming in a low pitch with your chin touching your chest. Slowly raise your chin upwards towards the ceiling. Somewhere in between you will find a comfortable point where your voice box "opens up" and your voice pitch sounds deep and rich. Perform a few sets around 20-30 seconds daily.

ALL ABOUT YOU

Write down 5 things you love about yourself.

1.
2.
3.
4.
5.

What would you tell your younger self in 5 words:

What is your biggest fear with transitioning?

Who has been the most supportive in your life?

Who is your biggest role model?

Where do you want to be in 5 years?

If your life was played as a song, what would it be?

What actor would play you in the movie about your life?

Say this out loud right now:
I know my worth. I am beautiful. I am loved. I'm not alone.

Name 3 things you are grateful for.

1.
2.
3.

What are the main areas in your life that you want to improve?

What will it take to improve those things?

Doodle something that makes you happy:

Say this out loud right now:
I take the lessons and the happiness from my past and leave the rest behind. This is my journey to be my best self. I am worthy.

MY JOURNEY

In late 2008, I embarked on a journey to find ways to transition from female to male naturally. Through many trials and error, I found that natural transitioning is possible.

The first changes I noticed were a decrease of fat and increased muscle tone. I started to grow sideburns and acquire chin hair. My facial shape become more masculine and I also noticed my hips were narrowing. My voice deepened with the help of voice exercises.

The first year, I still struggled with being called ma'am, she, her and female pronouns when out in public. I felt very discouraged and as if all of my hard work was in vain. Soon enough, I was able to "pass" more and had to start using the men's restroom. That was overwhelming at first, not to mention scary. I was terrified a man would peek into my bathroom stall. Might sound ridiculous, but it was a fear I had.

In 2010, I informed my boss at work I was transitioning from female to male, and requested the use of male pronouns at work. I was fortunate enough to have a very understanding workplace. This was the year I also had sex-reassignment surgery and became legally male. I still had never used synthetic testosterone, not even once.

In early 2011, I interviewed at new jobs as male and was hired as a marketing director at a rather conservative company. I completely passed at work and it was amazing to be myself without people ever knowing my sex at birth was female. I was able to see men and communicate with them on a much different level than ever before.

In December of 2011, I decided to try out testosterone injections. After three years of NT, I felt the next level of my journey was due. I remain overwhelmed by my amazing success with NT and still continue to see others worldwide experience the same, if not better, results.

Shortly after taking injections, my voice dropped almost immediately and more facial and body hair started to grow. I got horrific cystic acne all over my face, chest, shoulders and back. My face was too senstive to touch. That was a downfall. The next thing I realized was hair loss. I started to notice a receding hairline and my crown area was thinning. I would see hair shedding in my shower and my pillow.

Between the acne and the hair loss I grew alarmed. I decided after 6 months to cut my dosage of testosterone in half. It is now late summer of 2015, I have been using testosterone for almost 4 years and still take half of the prescribed dosage and experience the same results.

On a positive note, when I cut my testosterone in half, my acne went away and my hair loss slowed. I now use natural hair products and herbal supplements, such as saw palmetto, biotin and the Chinese herb Fo Ti, to aid with hair regrowth. One solution I suggest that has proven studies is using emu oil with minoxidil. Every night I apply emu oil to my scalp, then apply minoxidil. Within several weeks I noticed new hair growth and it felt revolutionary.

In 2013, I made the decision in my transition journey to become stealth. "Stealth" is virtually living your life as your authentic self without labeling yourself. I do not publically tell people I am transgender. Unless people are my family and friends, they do not know. I personally felt that it was time for me to simply live my life as I felt I was born to live it. I had spent 6 years of my life as a trans activist and leader of the social network, TQ Nation. My life was on display. I decided to hand over the torch to others ready to take over. Some of my greatest rewards in this life has been helping others with their journey.

There are no photos of me in this book because of being stealth. We all have a different journey. It is very personal and we must respect whatever each of us choose as our path.

I have gone through many degrees of challenges on my journey, yet have grown in magnificent ways. I learned to "know my worth" and to truly love myself. That in itself is priceless.

A DOCTOR'S CONCLUSION

I met Tristan one year at a Southern Comfort Conference. When I discovered in casual conversation that Tristan had never had an injection of testosterone, I was baffled. He told me about the regime he followed, the research he used, and we threw some ideas and opinions back and forth. Shortly thereafter I returned home to Toronto with renewed inspiration to continue this plight in the Far North.

Some patients, for reasons varying from liver disease to personal preference, cannot or will not take hormones. These patients still desire to masculinize their physical characteristics, and are seeking alternatives. In my own private practice as a Naturopathic Doctor, I use treatments that differ in certain ways from Tristan's, but ultimately we are all dedicated to the same cause, and I have developed the utmost respect for him. The countless hours he has invested in creating awareness for Trans Health issues is astonishing, and all for the simple purpose of reaching out to others.

The great thing about employing Naturopathic Medicine to assist in gender transitioning is that it can be used in several ways, and customized for the individual. I have prescribed natural substances alone to facilitate change, and I have also used them in conjunction with testosterone to decrease the negative side effects (acne anyone?). This whole process must be done under doctor supervision – never self-prescribe supplements! Certain substances may not be compatible with medications or supplements you are taking, or might even exacerbate certain health conditions.

Tristan is one of the most amazing people I have had the pleasure of meeting. He has made his experience widely available to the trans community, with little desire for fame, fortune, or credit, but rather simply to assist people who, like Tristan, are looking for alternatives to hormonal transitioning. He is truly an innovator in the field, stepping outside the box of conventional medicine, and although his process may not apply to everyone, he is certainly opening people's minds to something he is passionate about.

This book is monumental for the trans community. I would like to say that I am proud to know Tristan, and I would like to thank him personally for all of his hard work and dedication, and most of all for inspiring people like myself to join in his efforts.

Dr. Chelsea Derry, BSc, ND
Naturopathic Doctor
Ontario, Canada

ABOUT THE AUTHOR

Tristan Skye is the founder of TQ Nation™ and Natural Transitioning™.

Tristan was voted "Best Transgender Rights Activist" by the readers of *Southern Voice* (2009) and *The GA Voice* (2010 and 2011). He proudly led the second annual Trans March at Atlanta Pride (2010).

Tristan was also voted as one of Atlanta's most influential members of the LGBT community in the "Fenuxe Fifty" edition of *Fenuxe Magazine* (2010).

Tristan is honored to have cameo appearances in the ground-breaking documentaries, **Becoming Chaz** (2011) and **Trans** (2012).

Lastly, Tristan has been published multiple times as a guest writer for *Labrys Magazine* and *The GA Voice*.

www.ingramcontent.com/pod-product-compliance
Lightning Source LLC
Chambersburg PA
CBHW070339290526
45791CB00003B/1393